Math Around the Calendar

A Year's Worth of Seasonal Activities For Beginning Math Students

By Veronica Terrill

Fearon Teacher Aids
A Division of Frank Schaffer Publications, Inc.

Dedication
To my dear friend, Ty.
I'm glad we're walking
the same path.

Senior Editor: Kristin Eclov

Editor: Janet Barker

Illustrator: Veronica Terrill

Cover and Interior Design: Good Neighbor Press, Inc. Grand Junction, CO

Fearon Teacher Aids products were formerly manufactured and distributed by American Teaching Aids, Inc., a subsidiary of Silver Burdett Ginn, and are now manufactured and distributed by Frank Schaffer Publications, Inc. FEARON, FEARON TEACHER AIDS, and the FEARON balloon logo are marks used under license from Simon & Schuster, Inc.

© Fearon Teacher Aids

A Division of Frank Schaffer Publications, Inc.

23740 Hawthorne Boulevard

Torrance, CA 90505-5927

FE7978

ISBN 0-7682-0056-3

Table of Contents

Table of Contents

© Fearon Teacher Aids FE7978

Introduction

The seasons bring many fun and exciting opportunities to teach math concepts in ways that young children will enjoy and remember. *Math Around the Calendar* is a fun and practical classroom resource to help kindergarten, first, and second grade teachers reinforce math concepts using familiar seasonal and holiday themes.

Math Around the Calendar contains pages and pages of great ideas to help teachers easily add festive touches to addition, subtraction, time, and money math lessons. Activities and reproducible pages are adaptable to different age and skill levels. Pages can be changed before reproducing, adjusting the numbers and problems, as needed. Many of the activity pages can be completed with little or no teacher assistance, making *Math Around the Calendar* a great addition to homework packets or substitute teacher folders.

Math Around the Calendar also contains clever ideas for math games and directions for easy-to-make manipulatives and math centers. Seasonal math folder covers are also included!

From fall's "School Bus Table Game" to summer's "Sea Shell Store," get ready to celebrate math around *your* classroom all year long!

Have a fun year!

Veronica Terrill

Fall Math

Name_____

Folder Cover

Reproducible

Fall
Math Newsletter

Hi Parents!

_____

_____

_____

_____

_____

_____

_____

_____

_____

Home Math Helpful Hints

Here are some hints to make math homework go smoothly:

- Set aside the same time each day to work on math homework or extra math problems.
- The homework area should be quiet and well-lit.
- Have supplies handy; plenty of paper, sharpened pencils, rulers, etc.
- Be ready to answer questions or help, but let your child try to work the problem first.
- Keep completed homework in a visible spot near the door so it will be remembered.

Ideas to Try

Simple everyday tasks can help reinforce basic math skills that your child is learning at school. If your child helps sort the laundry it teaches them how to put things into categories. Here are other chores that teach:

- Setting the table—counting, addition and subtraction
- Cooking—measuring, time and fractions
- Shopping—money, counting, greater than, less than

Things to Count at Home

- [ ] doors
- [ ] windows
- [ ] beds
- [ ] chairs with arms
- [ ] chairs without arms
- [ ] TVs

2

Back-to-School

Bulletin Board

How to:

1. Cover the bulletin board background with brightly-colored paper.
2. Reproduce the patterns on pages 4 and 5. (Make additional labels for any activities you would like to illustrate.) Reproduce the clock pattern on page 103, and assemble with a brad. Color and/or cut out the patterns.
3. Label each apple with the correct time for each activity illustrated. Position the patterns on the board.
4. Use the clock to illustrate each activity time change, by moving the clock hands to match.

Reproducible

Back-to-School
Bulletin Board Pattern

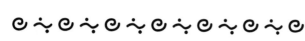

School starts
Recess
Lunch
Time to Go
Library
Math
Reading

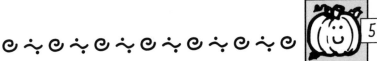

© Fearon Teacher Aids FE7978

Reproducible

Fall Math Center
Self-Check Stations

How to:

1. Cut a toilet paper roll to 2½" (6.2 cm). Cover one end with colorful paper. Write math problems on craft sticks with math problems and insert into the modified tube, as shown. Remove to check.

2. Measure 4" (10.2 cm) from one end of an 8½" x 11" (21 cm x 27 cm) sheet of heavy paper and fold at the 4-inch mark. Glue or staple the folded portion, forming a pocket, as illustrated. Insert the lettered craft sticks into the pocket. Remove to check.

3. Fold an index card in half. Write the math problem on the outside of the card and the answer on the inside. Flip the card open to check. The cards may be stacked together, in sets, or as desired.

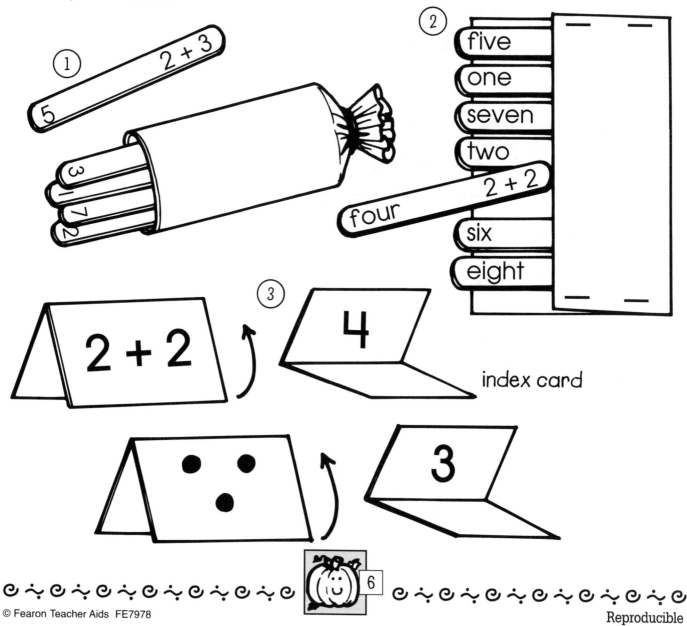

index card

Back-to-School
Bus Table Game

Teacher Instructions:

Cover a folded milk carton with yellow paper. Add bus details with a black marker, as illustrated. Reproduce the square shapes below and cut into individual pieces. Cover a large table with white paper. Make a random path from one end of the table to the other by gluing down the shapes (see illustration). Make a stack of squares for players to draw from. Move the "bus" from "school" to "home," by drawing a shape and advancing to the matching shape on the path.

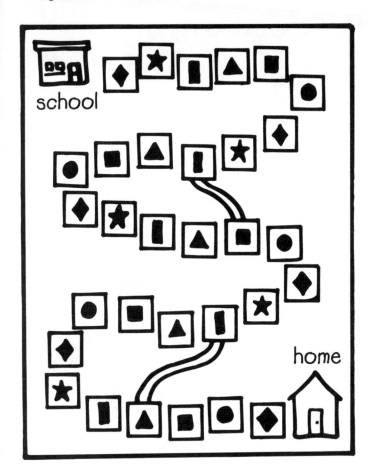

Challenge:

Have child tell the name of the shape in order. When correct, advance the bus. Reproduce several sets and cut apart at squares.

Shortcuts:

If you land on one you can advance to the next square connected to it.

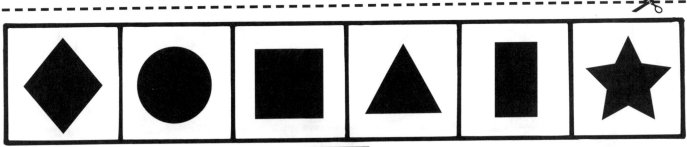

Reproducible

Fall

Teacher Helper: Parent Letter

Dear Parents,

We are collecting items for our math projects. Please help by saving any of the following items:

milk bottle caps

Styrofoam™ packing peanuts

Popcycle™ sticks

juice cans and lids (cleaned)

colored paper clips

We need the items by _____.
Thanks for your help.

Happy Fall!

_____
(teacher)

8

Name_____

Add:

Your age	+	Number of fingers on one hand	=	**?**

_____ + _____ = _____

Think!

What other number combinations can you use to make up your own math problems? What about your birthdate, plus your room number? How many problems can you make up?

9

Name_____

"Bizzy Bee" Math

Buzz around the classroom and count the following items:

Classroom Count

Let's Count!

How many students? _____

How many doors? _____

How many windows? _____

How many sinks? _____

How many tables? _____

How many flags? _____

How many pencil sharpeners? _____

10

Pencil Grouping

Pencils make wonderful and inexpensive manipulatives which are perfect for back-to-school counting. Cover orange juice cans with colorful paper. Using a bold, black marker, number the sides of the cans (by 2s, 5s, etc.), as shown. Fill large baskets with unsharpened pencils and place in the center of the table. Give each child a numbered can and have him or her fill it with the correct number of pencils. After checking, replace the pencils in the main basket and switch the cans around. Record results on page 12.

Name_____

Fall Manipulatives
Pencil Math

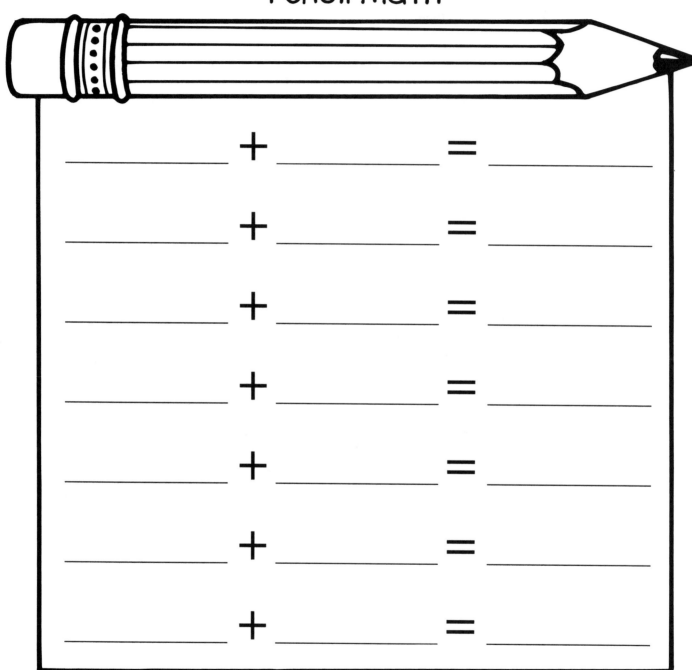

_____ + _____ = _____

_____ + _____ = _____

_____ + _____ = _____

_____ + _____ = _____

_____ + _____ = _____

_____ + _____ = _____

_____ + _____ = _____

✂ -

<u>Teacher Instructions:</u>

Use this page to have students create their own math worksheets. Have students pull a random number of pencils (or other manipulatives) and record that number in the first column. Take a second set of pencils and record the number in the second column. Have students find the sum.

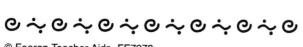

Learning My Number

Many teachers organize their classroom by assigning students numbers. Help them memorize their student number by creating personalized number tags using the pattern on page 14. Encourage students to be creative by using various designs and colors. Have students experiment on a separate sheet of paper. When they're satisfied with their drawing, have them transfer their best work to the pattern. Before placing finished product on student desks, laminate for durability. The numbers can be used year after year.

Reproducible

This Is My Number

My Name

fold -

This Is My Number:

14

Fall
Leaf Shape Sort and Graph

Reproduce the following leaf patterns selecting different colored paper for each shape. Duplicate each pattern five to ten times per child. Cut out, and laminate, if desired. Place all the leaves in a decorated bag and have each child draw the same number of leaves. "Rake" up a specific number of leaves and challenge children to try to match it.

Graph results: by color, by shape.

Leaf patterns

Reproducible

Name_____

Fall

Add-on Scene

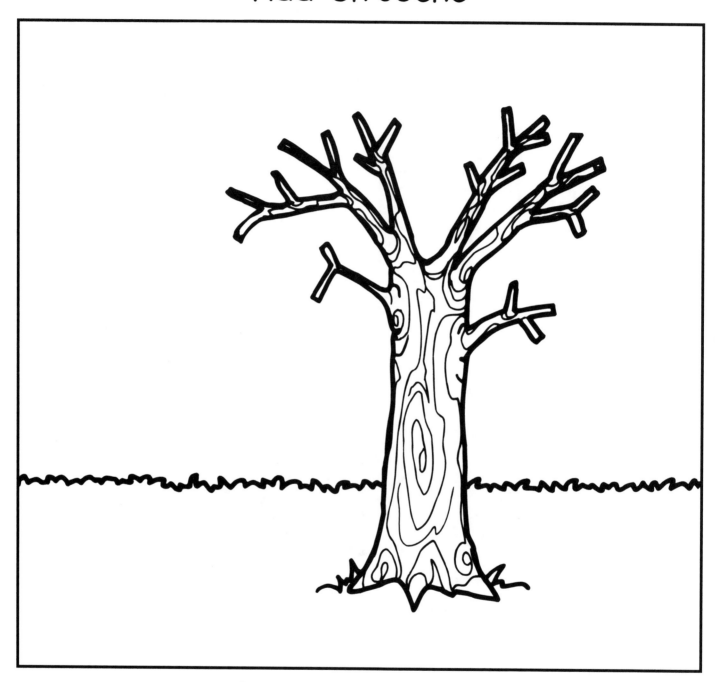

- Draw 6 leaves on the tree.
- Draw 1 sun in the sky.
- Draw 3 pumpkins on the ground.
- Draw 2 clouds in the sky.
- Draw 4 apples on the tree.

16

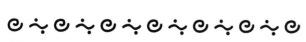

Reproducible

Name_____

Grandparent's Day

Stamp-a-Pattern Necklace

Help granny put on her necklace by making a fingerprint necklace. Push your index finger on a stamp pad, then, while your finger is still wet, create a bead print necklace around granny's lace bib. Try making a rainbow necklace by using different colored stamp pads.

Name_____

Columbus Day

Missing Number Fill-in

Can you spot the missing numbers?

 A 1, 2, ____, 4, 5, ____, ____, 8

 B 6, ____, 8, 9, ____, 11, ____, 13, 14

 C 1, ____, ____, 4, ____, 6, 7, 8, ____, 10

 D 3, ____, 5, ____, 7, 8, ____, 10

 E 2, 3, ____, 5, ____, 7, 8, 9

 F 4, ____, ____, 7, 8, 9, ____, ____

 G 5, 6, ____, 8, ____, ____, 11, 12

18

Name_____

Pumpkin Tooth Count

Can you count how many teeth each jack-o-lantern has?

_____   _____   _____

_____   _____   _____

Reproducible

Halloween
Navy Bean Ghosts

How to:

Create cute Halloween manipulatives by spray-painting navy or large-sized beans white or "spooky" glow-in-the-dark green. Draw eyes and mouth, as shown, using a black waterproof marker. For durability, laminate the haunted house scene below, and use as a math game board. Create simple math games such as: "Put three ghosts on the house. Take one ghost away. How many are left?" Formulate questions that challenge various skill levels. For safety's sake, be cautious when using small manipulatives around young children.

Name_____

Halloween
Spider Math

How to draw a spider:

  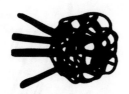 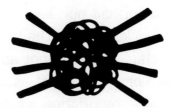

1 Scribble a body.

2 Draw a set of four legs on one side.

3 Draw another set of four legs on the other side.

8 legs in all!

- Draw 2 spiders on the web.
- Don't forget to draw 8 (eight) legs!
- How many sets of four legs did you draw?

21

Thanksgiving
Self-Check Turkey Math

How to:

Reproduce the pattern below on heavy, tan-colored paper. Color as desired and cut out. Fold on the dotted line creating a pocket behind the turkey. Staple sides. To keep craft sticks upright and for added stability, staple along the pocket as shown. Make craft stick "feathers" by printing math problems across the end. Write the answers on the end that's tucked into the pocket, as illustrated.

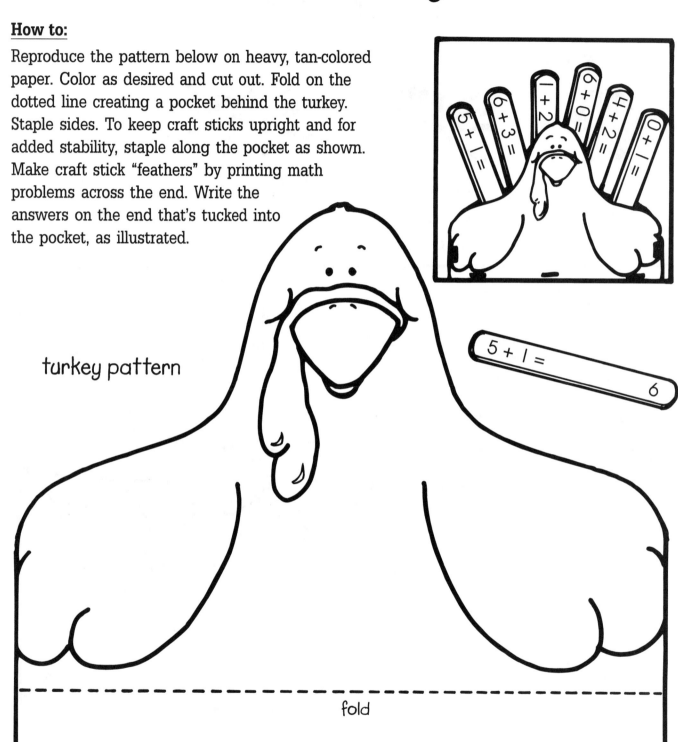

turkey pattern

fold

staple   staple   staple   staple   staple   staple

22

Reproducible

Name_____

Thanksgiving
Turkey Dinner Count

Circle the number of objects to match each number.

2	🌽 🌽 🌽 🌽 🌽
5	🥣 🥣 🥣 🥣 🥣
1	🍗 🍗 🍗 🍗 🍗
4	🥧 🥧 🥧 🥧 🥧
3	🍞 🍞 🍞 🍞 🍞
5	🍲 🍲 🍲 🍲 🍲
4	🫕 🫕 🫕 🫕 🫕

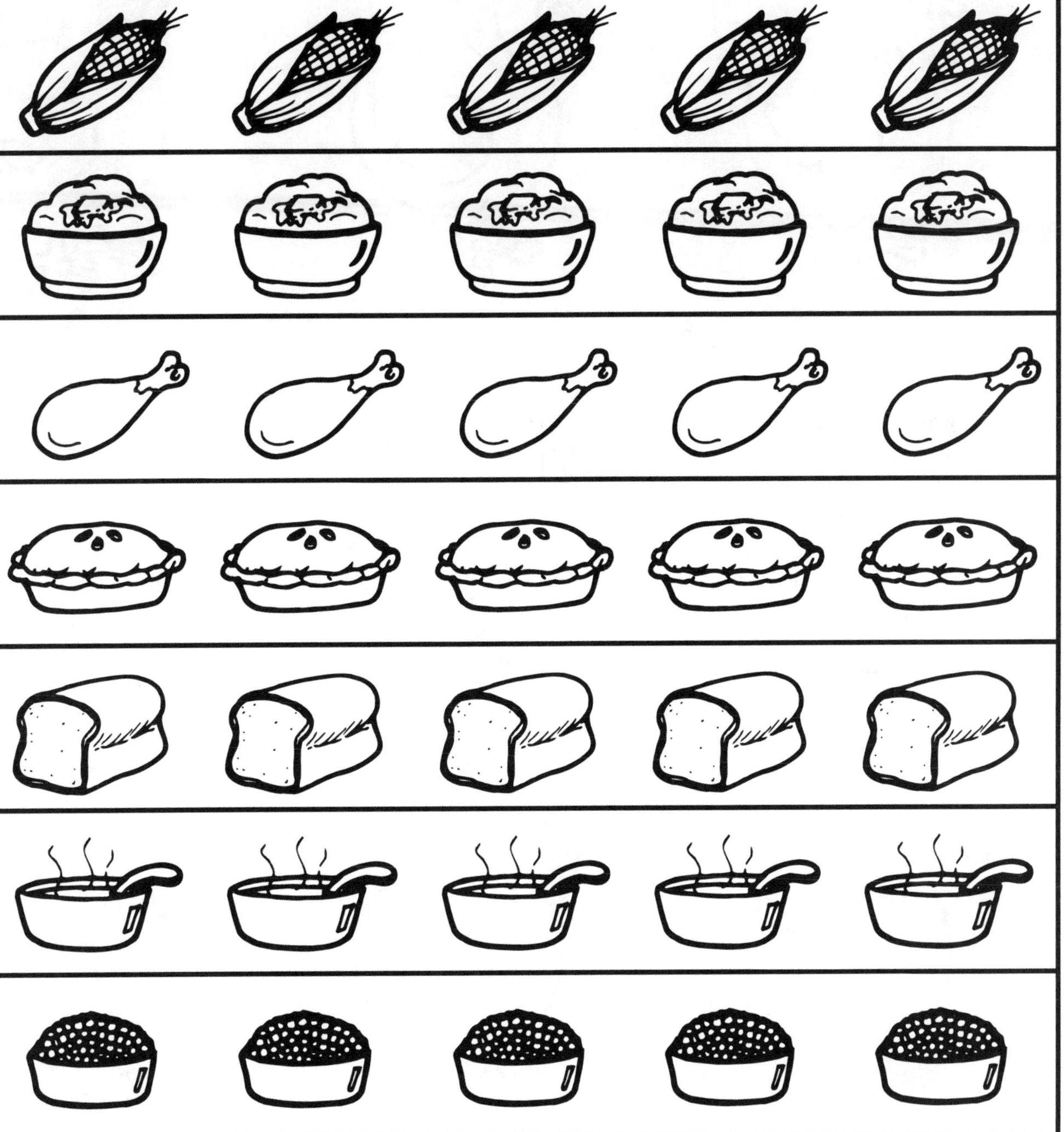

23

Reproducible

Name_____

Turkey Feather Match

Draw the correct number of feathers on each turkey.

2   6   3

7   1   5

4   8   2

24

Fall
Math Clip Art

MATH

HOMEWORK

M A T H

1 2 3 4
5 6 7 8
9 0 + −

Math Awards

Fold and staple onto student's work

Math Work
Sign, review, and return

_____
parent's signature

Be "Leaf"
It!
I'm Tops in Math!

_____

is "falling" for math!
Good work!

signed _____ date _____

WINTER MATH

Name_____

Folder Cover

27

Reproducible

Winter

Math Newsletter

Dear Parents,

_____

_____

_____

_____

_____

_____

_____

Happy Holidays!

_____

Let's Make Cookies!

Making cookies with your child is a great way to practice counting and measuring skills. Find a favorite recipe and show your child how the ingredients are listed and how to measure them using cups, teaspoons, etc. Practice counting the eggs, cups of flour, even the number of cookies the recipe makes. This is also a great time to talk about temperature. Best of all, you get to eat your homework!

Winter Patterns

1 • 3 • 1 • 3 • 1 • 3 • 1

Cranberry Popcorn Strings

These easy-to-make holiday garlands help your child practice counting and pattern skills. Thread alternating pieces of popcorn with fresh cranberries using heavy thread and a dull-tipped darning needle. Let your child choose the pattern and make different patterns for each string.

Snowman Count

How many?

eyes	☐
nose	☐
hat	☐
buttons	☐

28

Winter

Holiday Countdown Bulletin Board

Happy Holidays

Only ② days 'til winter break!

How to:

1. Cover the background of the bulletin board using seasonal colors, such as green and red. Wrapping paper also looks good.

2. Reproduce the ornament patterns found on page 30, enlarging or reducing to fit tree size. Consider varying the color and also the number of ornaments. Number each ornament from "1" to whatever number you will be counting down to.

3. Attach ornaments to the tree, as illustrated. Encourage children to take turns putting the ornaments on the board, adding one each day. Add any other caption, as desired.

Winter
Bulletin Board Patterns

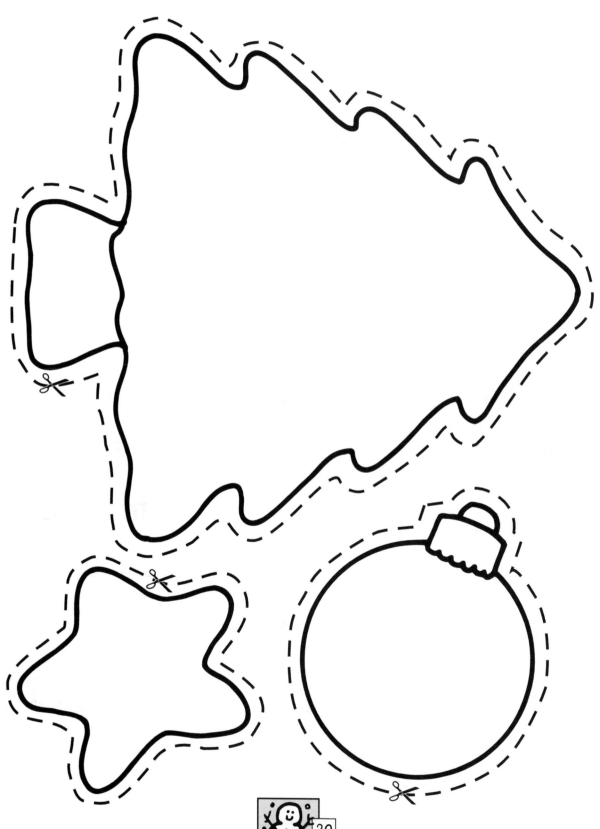

Reproducible

Winter

Math Center: Measure Me!

Teachers Instructions:

Reproduce the candy cane "rule" below, and winter patterns on page 32 and laminate for durability. Using the candy cane "ruler," have children measure each holiday object and record the measurements, either on the laminated cards or on a separate tally sheet. For additional measuring practice provide varying lengths of colorful ribbon or yarn to measure. For a variation, cut shapes out of wrapping paper and glue to heavy card stock.

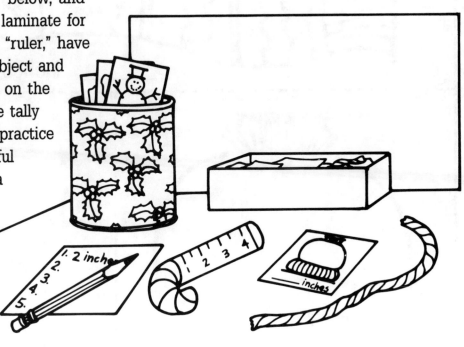

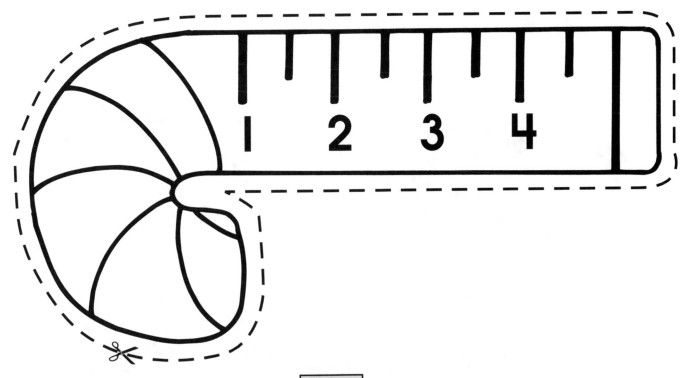

31

Reproducible

Winter

Measure Me! Patterns

_____ inches

_____ inches

_____ inches

_____ inches

_____ inches

32

Reproducible

Dice "Read-a-Number" Math Game

Hundreds 100	Tens 10	Ones 1
____	____	____
____	____	____
____	____	____
____	____	____
____	____	____
____	____	____
____	____	____
____	____	____
____	____	____
____	____	____
____	____	____

Object:
To create random 3-place numbers to practice reading numbers.

How to:
Roll a die to find a number for each column. When all three boxes in a column are filled, the second child tries to read the number out loud.

Bonus:
What is the largest and smallest number on each sheet?

Note:
For early math, hundreds columns may be removed before reproducing.

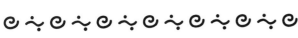

33

Teacher Helper

Pocket Shape Sorter

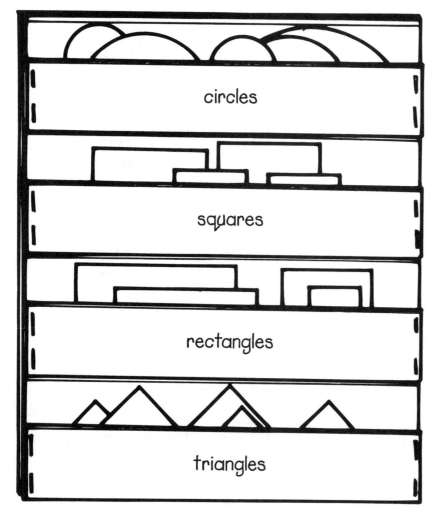

How to:

Use an 8½" x 11" (21 cm x 27 cm) sheet of heavy paper for a base. Cut two 8½" x 11" (21 cm x 27 cm) sheets of paper in half. Fold each half-sheet in half again, as illustrated. Staple each folded section to the base sheet of paper. Label each pocket with "circles," "squares," etc.

For very young children:

Illustrate each pocket with an example. Reproduce the shapes below on colorful card stock or laminate for durability. Vary the sizes and color while reproducing. Shapes may also be cut from wrapping paper or wallpaper samples. Challenge children to sort shapes, placing like shapes into the correct pocket.

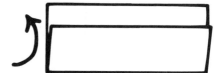

shape patterns (vary sizes while reproducing)

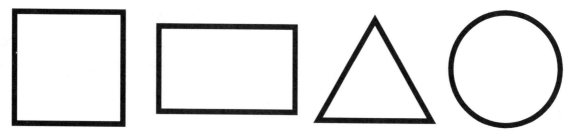

Reproducible

Name_____

Winter
"Brain Teezer"

Can you add your phone number?

___ ___ ___   Write the first three numbers here.

+ ___ ___ ___ ___   Write the last 4 numbers here.

___ ___ ___ ___ ___   What is the total?

Who has the largest number in the class? _____

Who has the smallest? _____

How many odd numbers? _____

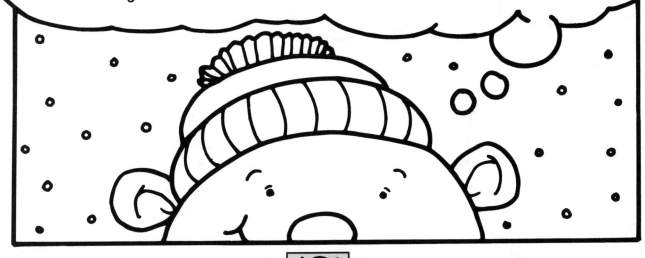

35

Name_____

Winter

"Bizzy Bee" Math

Let's follow directions!

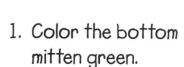

1. Color the bottom mitten green.

2. Draw 3 yellow stars on the top mitten.

3. Draw 6 red circles on the mitten that's left without designs. Color the circles red.

4. When you are done, cut out and use as bookmarks.

Teacher hint:
After the mittens are colored, cut them out to use as classroom decorations or bookmarks.

Winter Manipulatives
Cotton Ball Santa

For each child:

Reproduce the pattern on page 38, and color as desired. Fill large plastic bowls or boxes with cotton balls, 20 for each child.* After skills practice, have children glue one cotton ball to each number to complete Santa's beard. Use the cotton ball to practice grouping skills, making groups of 2, 5, and 10.

*Provide each child with a small paper bag or container to hold the cotton balls.

Count out 20

2 groups of 10 cotton balls

4 groups of 5 cotton balls

10 groups of 2 cotton balls

Name_____

Winter Manipulatives
Santa Pattern

 38

Name_____

Winter

Add-on Winter Scene

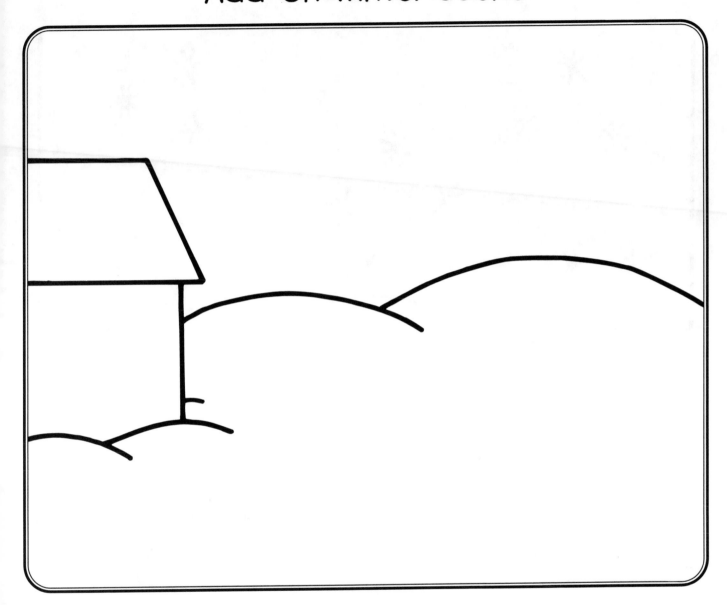

- Draw 2 trees on the hill.

- Draw 1 window on the house.

- Draw 3 snowmen in the yard.

- Draw 6 snowflakes in the sky.

- Draw 1 chimney on the roof.

 39

Name_____

Winter

Snowflake Sets

- Circle each set of 3 snowflakes.
- How many sets of 3? _____
- How many sets of 6 can you make? _____
- How many snowflakes in all? _____

40

<u>Winter</u>

Teeny Tiny Snowmen

Practice counting, and following directions skills with "Teeny Tiny" Snowmen. Pour a small amount of white poster paint into a jar lid or use a white stamp pad. Give each student a piece of dark blue or black construction paper and several cotton swabs. Have them fold the paper into fourths. Following the teacher's instructions, students will number each square with a white crayon and make the correct number of snowmen in each, using the cotton swab to "dab" each section, as illustrated. Add faces with black pen or marker. When the paint is dry and math directions are completed, students may create snowmen scenes using crayons or stickers.

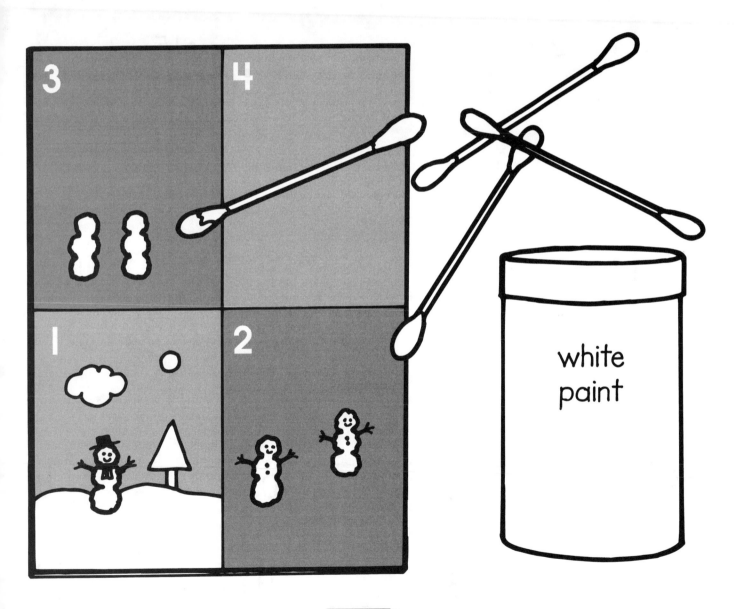

Reproducible

Winter

Count, Color, and Decorate

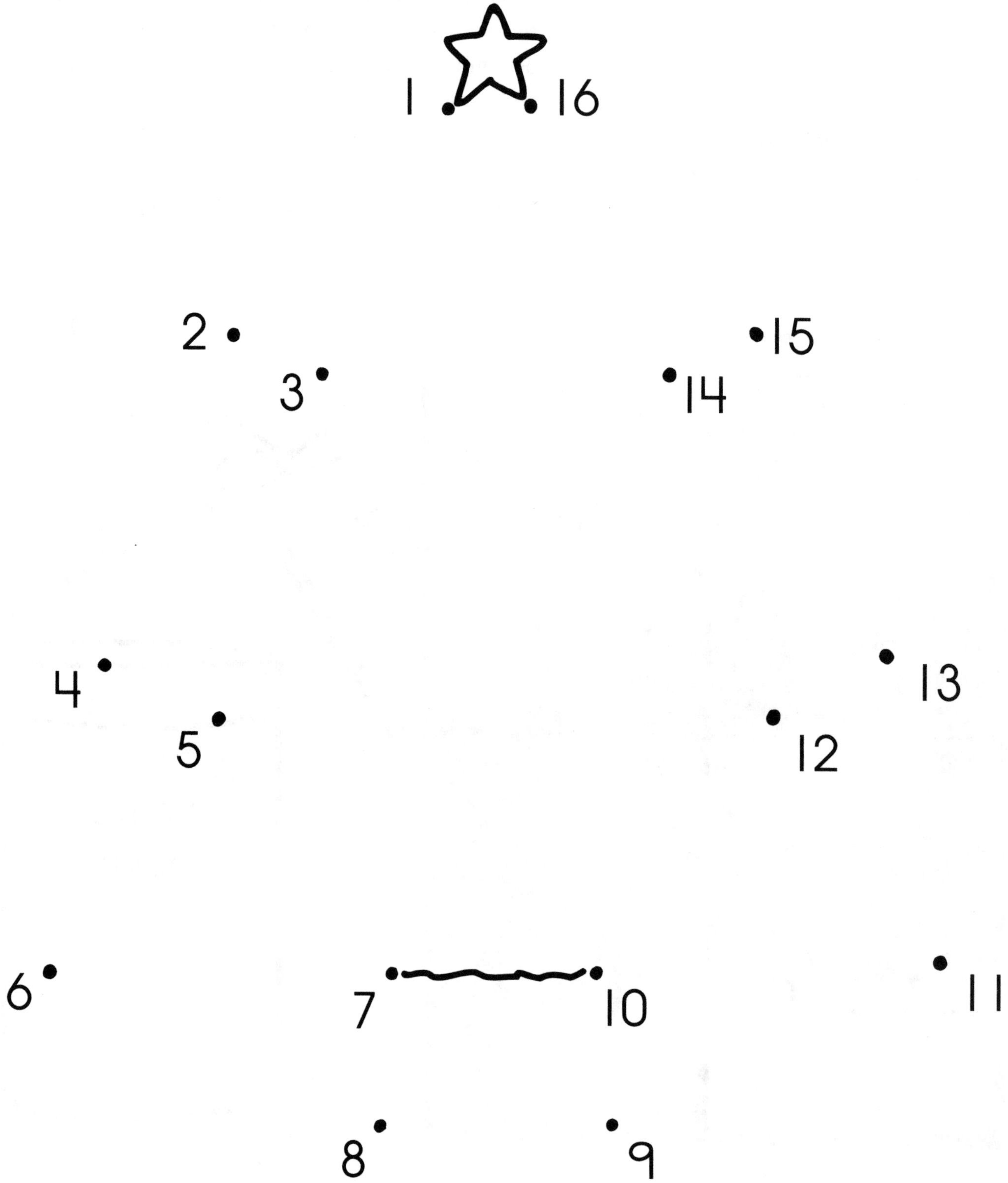

1 ✦ 16

2 •

3 •

•15

•14

4 •

5 •

•13

•12

6 •

7 •━━━━━━━• 10

•11

8 •

9 •

42

Name_____

Winter

Ornament Count

Use small stamps, stickers, or a pencil eraser (the tip makes a nifty, and thrifty, circle stamp) and stamp pad to decorate each tree with the correct number of "ornaments," as shown, on tree trunk.

43

Name_____

Hanukkah

Finish the Menorah

Finish drawing candles on the menorah. It needs 8 more. Put $\frac{1}{2}$ of the candles on the right side of the middle candle, and the other $\frac{1}{2}$ on the left side.

44

Reproducible

Name_____

Kwanzaa
"First Fruits" Count

Kwanzaa means "first fruits of the harvest." Count the fruit in each basket and write the number in the spaces below.

_____   _____   _____

_____   _____   _____

_____   _____   _____

45

Name_____

New Year's Day
Balloon Fractions

① Color $\frac{1}{2}$ of the balloons blue. ② Color $\frac{1}{4}$ of the balloons yellow.

③ Color the rest of the balloons red.

Chinese New Year
Macaroni Dragons

Reproduce the pattern below for each child. Color and cut out. Fold dragon in half, as indicated. With glue, attach a brightly-colored piece of yarn, about 8–12" (20–30 cm) long, to dragon's head. Give child a bag of assorted colored macaroni or colored beads. Instruct children to create a dragon's body, stringing the macaroni into patterns. When finished allow to dry, then reinforce with tape, stringing, glue a folded piece (2" square or 5 cm) of red construction paper to the dragon's tail to prevent beads from sliding off.

Finished
Project

Pattern

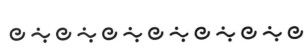

Reproducible

Ground Hog Day
Shadow Measure Comparison

Draw a circle around the ground hog with the <u>shortest</u> shadow.

1.

2.

3.

Draw a circle around the ground hog with the <u>longest</u> shadow.

4.

5.

6.

Valentine's Day
Big, Bigger, Biggest Hearts

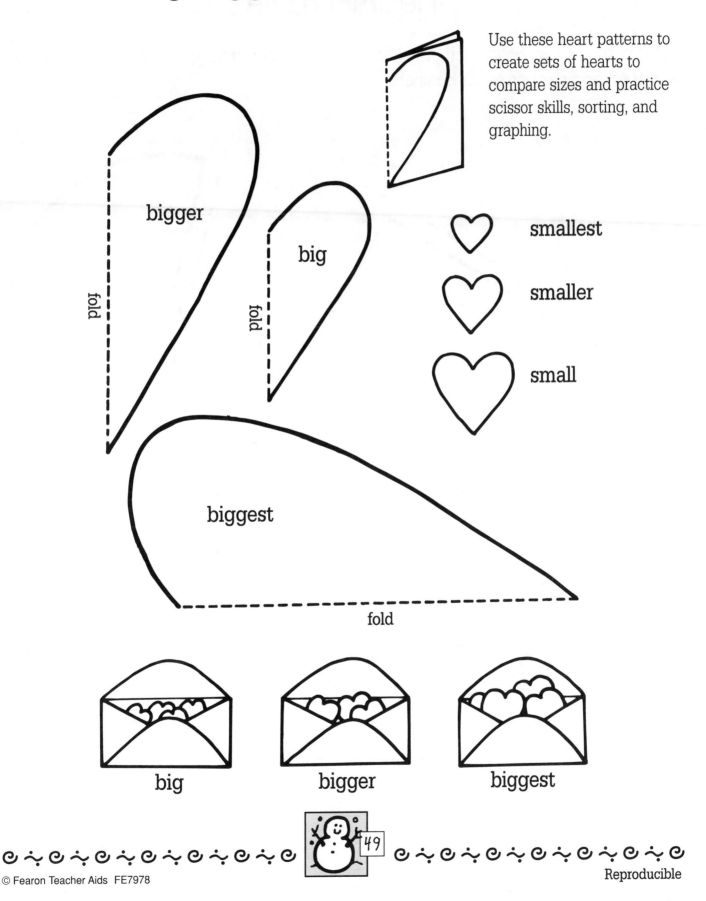

Use these heart patterns to create sets of hearts to compare sizes and practice scissor skills, sorting, and graphing.

bigger

big

fold

fold

smallest

smaller

small

biggest

fold

big

bigger

biggest

Valentine's Day
Heart Puzzle

Cut out the pieces below. Fit them together to make a heart. Glue to a red piece of paper and decorate, as desired.

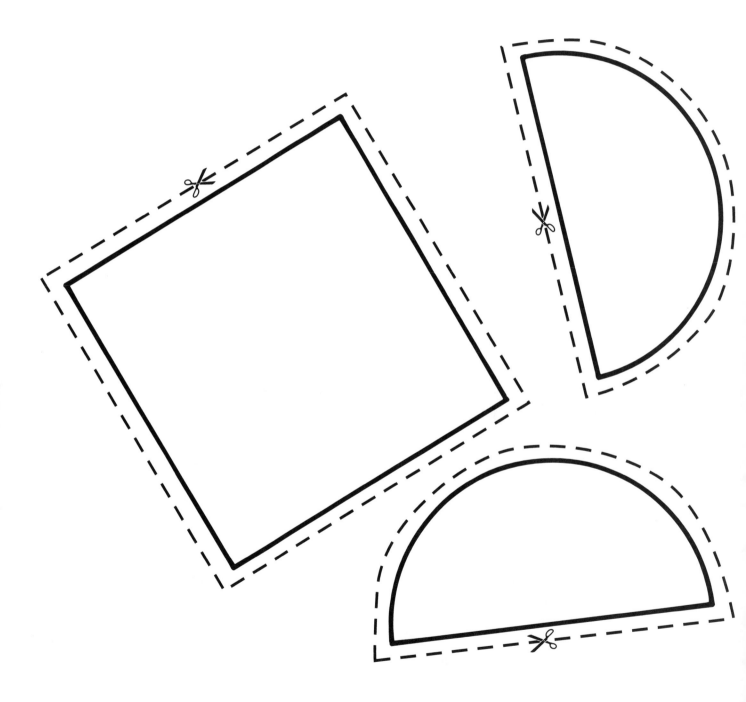

President's Day
Penny and Quarter Fun

<u>Teacher Instructions:</u> The following three activities work well as math center lessons.

Heads or Tails?

Each child gets a coin. Have each child mark his or her guess (heads or tails) before they flip their coin. Graph guesses and results.

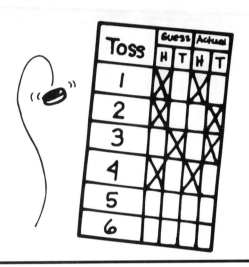

How many pennies will fit?

Give each child a margarine lid and have them guess "How many pennies will fit in the space without overlapping?" Count the pennies then place in lid. How many, more or less, did it really take?

Try other lid types and sizes.

Let's Make Sets

25 pennies equals 1 quarter. How many different sets can you make with 25 pennies (5s, 10s etc.)? How about 50 or 100 pennies?

Reproduce these on heavy paper and laminate if desired or use real money or plastic coins.

Reproducible

Winter
Math Clip Art

Math Rules!

Math Is Cool!

greater than  less than

Happy Holidays!

52

Winter
Math Awards

Fold and staple onto student's work

Math Work
Look what we've been up to!
Please review, sign and return.
Thanks!

_____
parent's signature

Math Award

Happy "Holly" days!

(certificate)

"Snow" body's better in math than

_____

_____   _____
signed   date

© Fearon Teacher Aids FE7978

Reproducible

SPRING MATH

Name_____

54

Spring
Math Newsletter

Happy Spring!

_____

_____

_____

_____

_____

Let's look at weather maps!

Weather maps are a wonderful resource to practice math basics with your child at home.

Try some of these activities:

- Find the hottest local and national temperatures.
- Find the coolest.
- Find the difference between the highest and lowest local temperatures.
- Compare the predicted high temperature for the day with the actual temperature listed in the next day's newspaper.

Spring Flower Count

In the space below help your child draw a spring flower with:

  1 stem, 6 petals, 3 leaves

Home Shape Search

Can you find these shapes at home? How many?

_____   _____

_____   _____

Reproducible

Spring
"April Fool" Math Bulletin Board

April Fool

7 + 3 = 10

10 < 5

3 > 1

triangle

circle

12 − 6 = 6

$$\begin{array}{r} 4 \\ + 6 \\ \hline 11 \end{array}$$

square

Did I Fool You?

three + one = four

How to:

1. Cover the bulletin board background with colorful paper. Reproduce patterns on pages 57 and 58, enlarging as needed to fit the space. Attach to the board, except the "Fool's Hat."

2. On varying sizes and shapes of paper, write out math problems, as illustrated. Some are correct, but others are to "April Fool" the children. Attach to the board. Place the fool's hat patterns in a plastic bag and attach to the bottom of the bulletin board, as shown.

3. When a child spots an "April Fool" problem, have them pin or tape a fool's hat on top of it.

4. Change the problems as desired.

56

Reproducible

April Fool

57

Did I Fool You?

Spring
Math Center Stamps

Stamps and ink pads are a wonderful resource to make unique math worksheets, counting cards, and other math activities. In a math center setting, provide various shapes and sizes of stamps with washable ink pads. Let the children make, and solve, their own math problems.

For example:

Suggested activities:

Counting cards:
- same object/same color
- different objects
- same object/different color

Make and solve:
Provide blank strips of paper with only +, –, and =, on it. Children will fill in.

Solve and stamp:
Provide number problems and let the children stamp their answers.

Reproducible

Spring
Playground Math Drawing

Take advantage of a beautiful spring day to practice graph drawing on the playground. Mark off a 9" square (22 cm) grid, as illustrated, with masking tape, washable paint or chalk. Reproduce copies of teacher-inspired drawings, making sure to keep the shapes as simple as possible. Give children a copy, along with a piece of chalk, and have them try to recreate the drawing. For surprising results, cut teacher copy into squares and distribute randomly for children to draw. Large sheets of cardboard may also be used for indoor work.

Note:

If you cut the squares apart, be sure to indicate the top of the design with a dot.

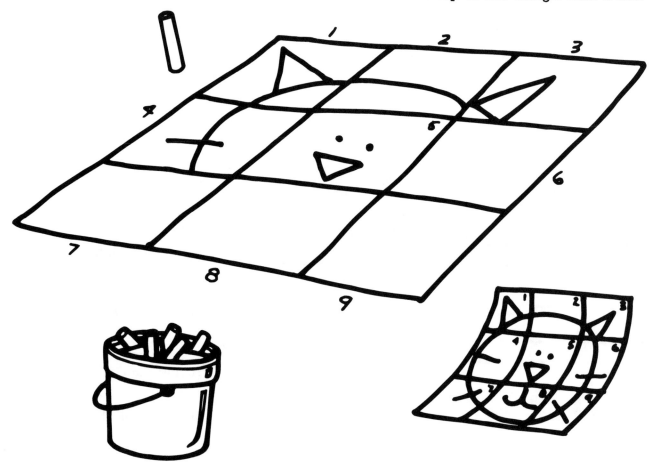

Reproducible

Spring
Clothespin Math

Brightly painted clothespins make great counting helpers. Spray-paint the clothespins assorted colors. Number clothespins or glue small, numbered cardboard squares on the end, as shown.

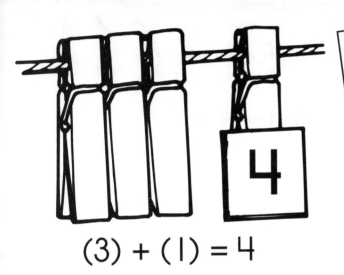

$(3) + (1) = 4$

Child finds "4" and clips it on.

Ideas for use:
- String clothespins together on a line.
- Clip to the side of a box.
- Draw random numbers to create problems.
- Use to follow story problems.

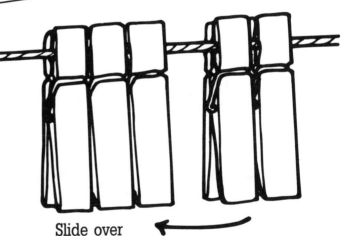

Slide over to count.

$3 + 2 = 5!$

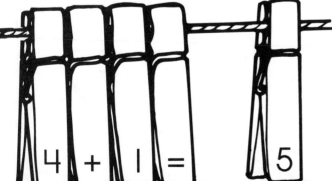

$4 + 1 =$ 5

61

© Fearon Teacher Aids   FE7978

Reproducible

Name_____

Spring
Brain Teezer

Story Problem

Bunny ate 1 carrot for breakfast.

Then bunny ate 4 carrots for lunch.

Finally bunny ate 3 carrots for dinner.

How many carrots did bunny eat in one day?

_____ + _____ + _____ = _____

Name_____

Spring
Bizzy Bee Math

Let's solve and color!

Answers:

1 or 2 = yellow   7 or 8 = blue

3 or 4 = red   9 or 10 = white

5 or 6 = green

5 + 5

6 + 1

2 + 1

1 + 1

2 + 3

5 + 0

2 + 4

5 + 1

6 + 3

3 + 3

3 + 2

63

Reproducible

Spring Manipulatives
Easter Egg Fractions

How to:

Using the pattern below, cut out egg shapes from brightly-colored or patterned heavy paper. If desired, laminate for durability. Cut the egg into various fractions and mix-up. Store in an envelope glued to the back of the basket pattern on page 65.

To use:

Have children remove egg sections and lay them, plain side up, on a table. Then, by matching the correct fractions, try to make a whole egg. Children can check results by turning sections over, to see if all the pieces match. (Label the fraction sections on the bottom to self-check.)

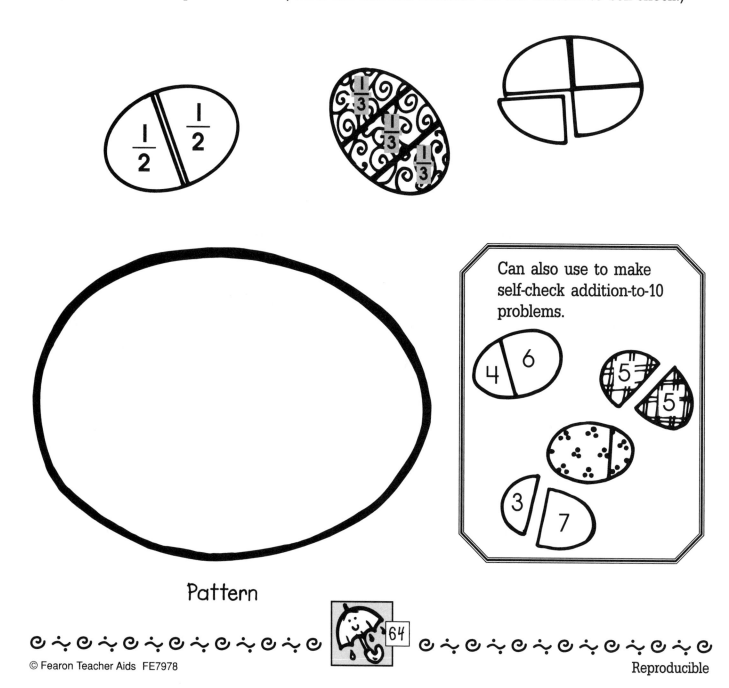

Can also use to make self-check addition-to-10 problems.

Pattern

Reproducible

Spring
Basket Pattern

back

Reproducible

Spring
Butterfly Measure Stick

How to:

Cut out four wings from the pattern below. Glue to the inside of large craft stick, as shown. For antenna, cut a pipe cleaner in half, curl one end and glue to the inside of craft stick. Glue a second craft stick over the wings and antenna to create body. Glue on a wiggle eye and draw a smile, as illustrated. Using a ruler add measure marks. Send children on a "scavenger" hunt with their butterfly measuring stick to see if they can find objects that are longer, shorter, same size, etc., as their stick. Conduct the hunt on the playground, classroom, or at home. Graph the results.

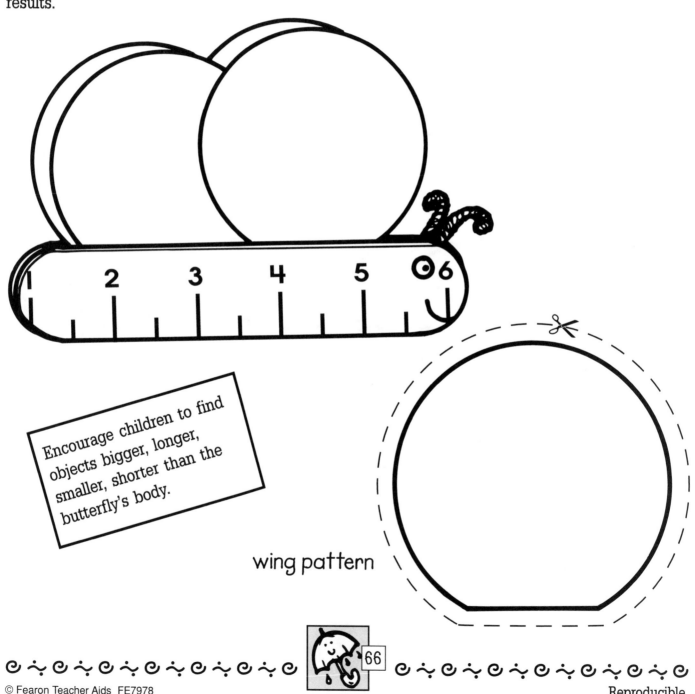

Encourage children to find objects bigger, longer, smaller, shorter than the butterfly's body.

wing pattern

Spring

Silly, Silly Recipes

Familarize children with measuring tools by creating silly recipes from random objects. Make up your own silly recipes or fill-in the "recipe" card below. Fold on the dotted line, leaving the "fill-in-the-blank" spaces facing up. Have students fill-in the blanks with creative ingredients. Open the paper and read the complete "recipe" displaying the measuring cups and spoons. (Remind children that these are silly, pretend, recipes not to be eaten.)

Recipe for Soup . . .

_____

Mix well: 2 cups of . . .

           $\frac{1}{2}$ cup of . . .

           2 teaspoons of . . .

Add: 1 Tablespoon of . . .

           1 pint of . . .

Stir well. Serves: . . .

_____ sound

_____ object at home

_____ object in room

_____ plant

_____ color

_____ big number

Display real measuring tools and provide dry rice or beans to practice measuring.

67

Reproducible

Name_____

Ladybug Count

How to:

Using a washable stamp pad or paint, "fingerpaint" a spot with your index finger.

When the ink or paint dries, use a black marker to add three dots on the bug and two "feelers" on the top, as shown.

Complete the activity below adding ladybugs to the flower.

Make 2 ladybugs.

Make 4 ladybugs.

Make 3 ladybugs.

How many ladybugs in all?

_____

68

Name_____

St. Patrick's Day
Shamrock Match

Draw a line and match the number to the correct set of shamrocks.

5

7

3

6

2

4

St. Patrick's Day
Gold Coin Count

Count the gold coins. Write your answer on the pot of gold.

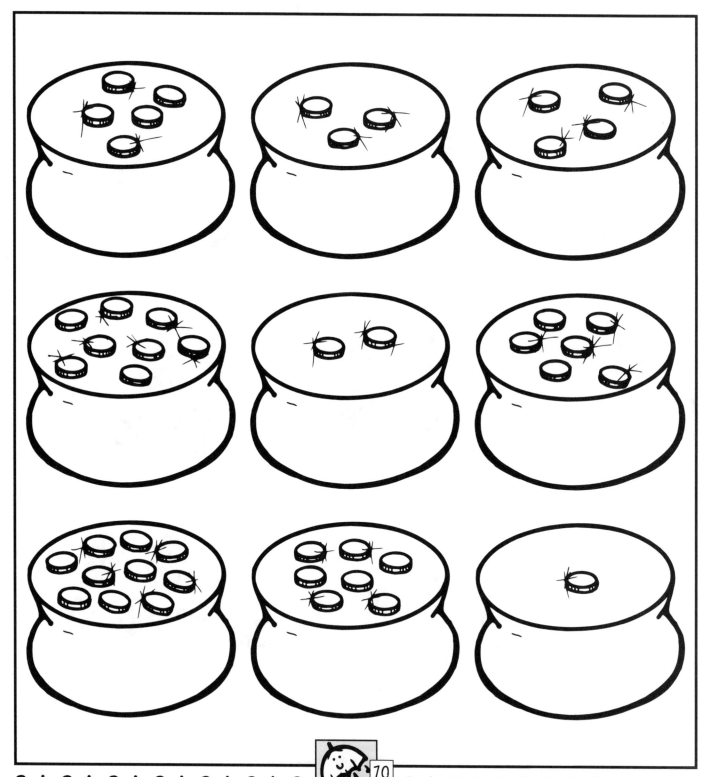

Easter
Bunny Hop Game

To play:

Cut out and color bunny markers, assigning each a different color. Children take turns rolling a die, moving their markers accordingly. Follow directions provided in each square. The first child to finish wins. For durability, laminate markers and gameboard.

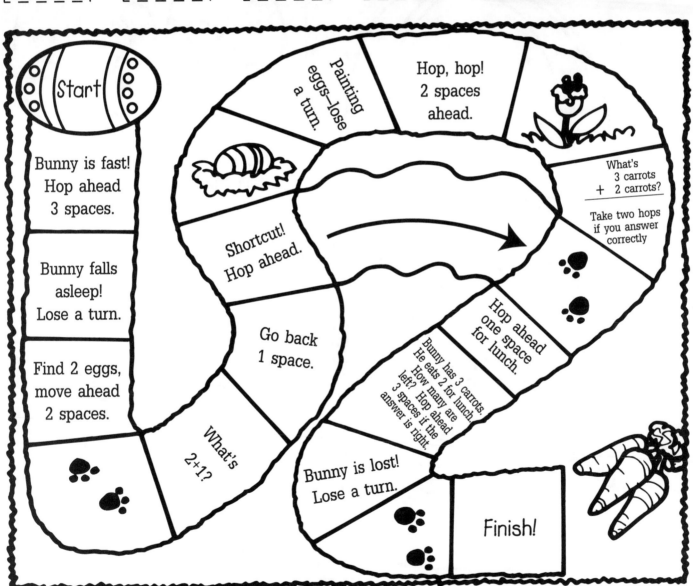

Start

Bunny is fast! Hop ahead 3 spaces.

Bunny falls asleep! Lose a turn.

Find 2 eggs, move ahead 2 spaces.

What's 2+1?

Go back 1 space.

Shortcut! Hop ahead.

Painting eggs—lose a turn.

Hop, hop! 2 spaces ahead.

What's 3 carrots + 2 carrots? Take two hops if you answer correctly

Hop ahead one space for lunch.

Bunny has 3 carrots. He eats 2 for lunch. How many are left? Hop ahead 3 spaces if the answer is right.

Bunny is lost! Lose a turn.

Finish!

 71

Reproducible

Easter Egg "Jelly" Bean Match

How to:

Spray-paint navy beans different colors. Place in a large bowl or shallow box. Have children pick an egg, then fill it with as many "jelly" beans as it takes to match the outside number. Switch eggs and have children check to see if beans and number correspond. Store the eggs in a straw-filled basket.

Number colored plastic Easter eggs, from 1 to 10, or as desired.

Name_____

Easter
"Finish-the-Line"

Fill-in the missing numbers.

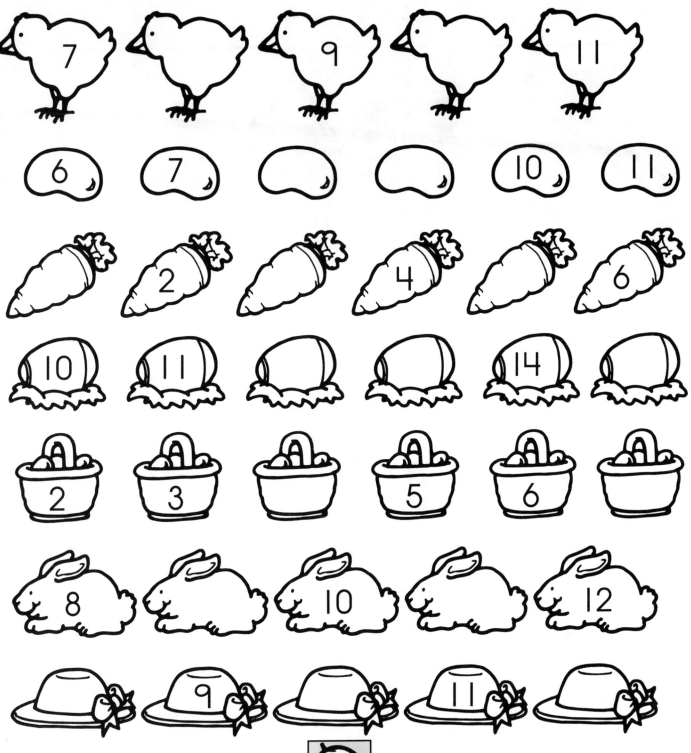

7   9   11

6   7   10   11

2   4   6

10   11   14

2   3   5   6

8   10   12

9   11

Name_____

Cinco de Mayo
Piñata Candy Count

Cinco means "5" in Spanish. How many sets of 5 can you find?
Find and circle each set of 5 candies.

How many sets of "5" did you find ? _____

74

Name_____

Mother's Day
Flower Match

Match the number of flowers in each pot to the correct number. Draw a line.

7

3

5

4

2

1

6

8

Reproducible

Patriotic Holidays

Decorate a Flag

Follow the directions below to create your own flag.

Draw 3 stars. Draw 0 stripes.

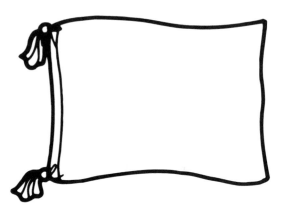

Draw 1 star. Draw 1 stripe.

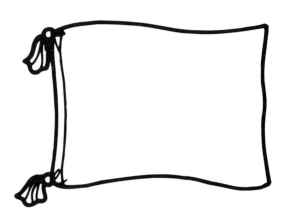

Draw 5 stars. Draw 2 stripes.

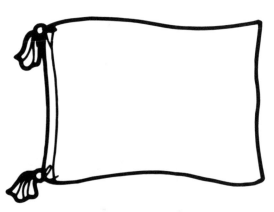

Draw 4 stars. Draw 3 stripes.

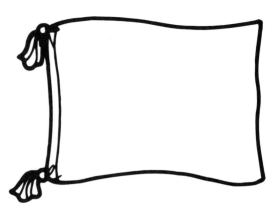

Draw 3 stars. Draw 3 stripes.

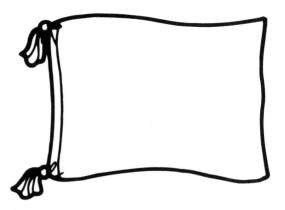

Draw 2 stars. Draw 4 stripes.

76

Reproducible

Patriotic Holidays
Sparkle Numbers

Draw your number on cardboard or tagboard using a thin line of white glue.

Sprinkle each number with red, white, or blue glitter.

Let dry. Shake off excess glitter.

Create these sparkle numbers to make dates and facts more memorable. Illustrate facts such as, "How many stars appear on the American flag?" and "What year was our country's birthday?" Older children can create their own birthdays, ages, and student number.

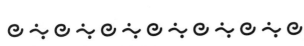

77

Reproducible

Spring
Math Clip Art

Our math work is flying high!

Kids Count

What's your estimate?

Save For My Portfolio!

1 2 3
4 5 6
7 8 9
0 + −

Spring
Math Awards

parent's signature

sign below and return by _____

fold

_____'s

work is
wonderful!

I did
"eggstra"
special in
math
today!

(certificate)

_____
name

is hopping right along in
Math!

_____ _____
signed   date

SUMMER MATH

Name_____

Folder Cover

Reproducible

Summer
Math Newsletter

Dear Parents,

_____

_____

_____

_____

_____

Have a Safe and Fun Summer!

P.S. Remember to practice your math facts!

Summer Math Fun

 Send a postcard to a friend or relative. Count the numbers in the address.

 Keep a graph of the daily high temperature for the week.

 Count and sort seashells according to shape, size, etc.

 Time and chart daily activities like brushing teeth and eating lunch.

Take-a-Trip Facts

When you travel this summer help your child keep a log of the following trip facts to practice math:

- How far in miles did we travel?
- How long did the trip take?
- How many stops? How many minutes per stop?
- How much did gas cost?

81

Summer
Math Bulletin Board

Cool Summer Math Facts

How many summer math facts can you "scoop" up?

How to:

1. Cover the bulletin board background with a bright summer color. Reproduce the patterns on pages 83 and 84, enlarging as necessary to fit the space. Reproduce the ice cream pattern on various colored papers.

2. Write homework assignments on ice cream scoops. Assignments should include math facts related to summer, such as the "Hottest temperature ever recorded," and "How many miles to the beach?" Give each child several of these "Ice Scream Scoops." This may also become a library research, or group project. Letter each scoop and attach each to a personalized cone, as illustrated. Who has the biggest ice cream cone?

82

Reproducible

Summer
Bulletin Board Pattern

How many summer math facts can you "scoop" up?

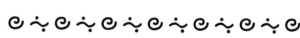

Reproducible

Summer
Math Center

The following activities can be set up in the math center for independent student discovery.

(1) Create multiple flip books using index cards, a felt-tip marker, a hole punch, and key rings. On the left side of an index card, write an addition or subtraction problem. On the far left side, write the answer. Fold back the answer as indicated. Problems can be grouped according to like numbers. When you have a set of problems, punch a hole in the upper left-hand corner, then link together using a key ring.

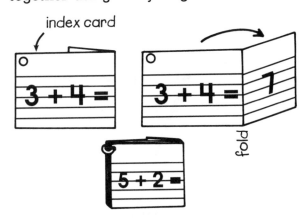

index card

fold

(2) Make a mini math poster flip chart using string, paper, tape, and drinking straws. Start with a brightly-colored 12" x 18" (30.5 cm x 45.7 cm) piece of heavy cardboard to use as the background. Securely tape to the back of the cardboard a piece of yarn, about 18" (45.7 cm). Take two wide drinking straws and thread a 15" (38.1 cm) piece of yarn through them.

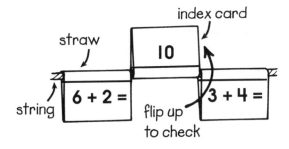

straw

index card

string

flip up to check

Tape yarn ends to the back of the cardboard making sure they're taut. Fold in half three pieces of 3" x 5 $\frac{1}{2}$" (7.6 cm x 14 cm) white paper and place over straws. Tape the bottom closed. Write addition problems on the front. Flip up and write answers on the back as shown. Repeat, creating five rows approximately 3" (3.6 cm) apart. Utilize the back of the poster with additional math facts.

(3) Assemble resealable plastic bags, index cards, a stapler, and felt-tip marker for a window flip book. Write math problems on one side of each index cards and the answer on the back. Place in resealable plastic bags. Group 12 math facts together, then staple along the top.

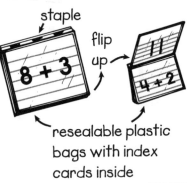

staple

flip up

resealable plastic bags with index cards inside

Summer
Father's Day

Is the number on the left greater than >, or less than < the number on the right?
Fill in the correct symbol.

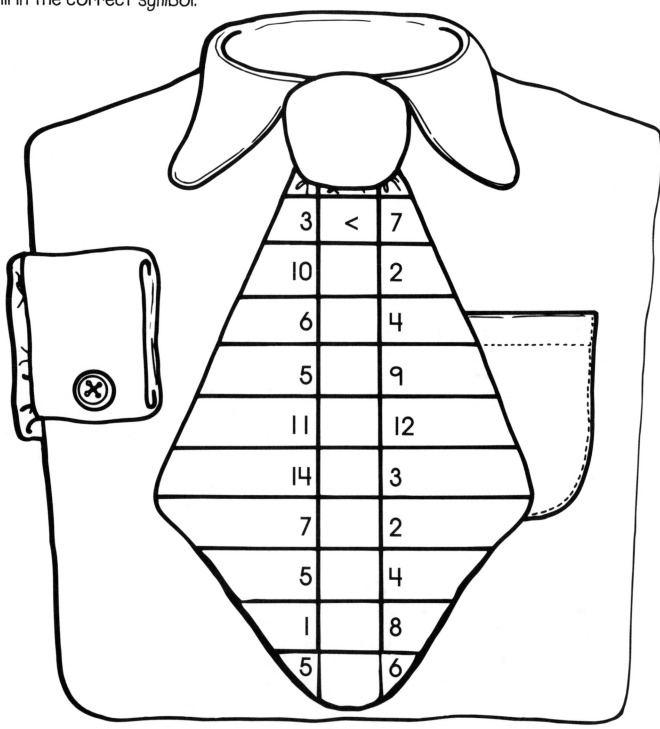

3	<	7
10		2
6		4
5		9
11		12
14		3
7		2
5		4
1		8
5		6

Reproducible

Teacher Helper: I "Can Do"

color-coded

I know my "7" facts.

3 + 7 = 10

Beth Can-Do

Use plastic containers with lids (such as margarine and frosting tubs) to organize and track progress in learning math facts. Give each student a plastic resealable bag containing math facts written on small strips of index card paper. As each fact is mastered, place the card in the "Can-Do" can. Check students' progress periodically to see if they really "can-do" the problems. When the bags are empty, reward students with a treat or a "can-do" party.

cut apart

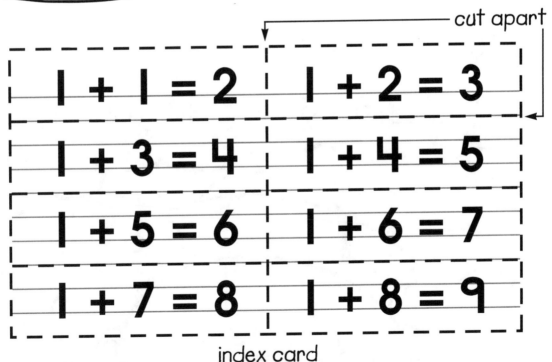

1 + 1 = 2	1 + 2 = 3
1 + 3 = 4	1 + 4 = 5
1 + 5 = 6	1 + 6 = 7
1 + 7 = 8	1 + 8 = 9

index card

Reproducible

Summer

"Brain Teezer"

Circle the missing + or − signs to make each problem true.

6 ___ 1 = 7   +   or   −

8 ___ 2 = 10   +   or   −

7 ___ 3 = 4   +   or   −

9 ___ 1 = 8   +   or   −

5 ___ 3 = 2   +   or   −

4 ___ 4 = 8   +   or   −

10 ___ 5 = 5   +   or   −

88

Name_____

Name_____

Summer
"Bizzy Bee" Math

In each column, fill in the missing **dots**, **numbers** and/or **letters**.

Let's read our numbers!

Dots	Numbers	Letters
•	1	o ___ e
•	2	two
• • •		three
• • • •	4	fo ___ r
⦙ • ⦙		five
⦙ ⦙	6	six
⦙ ⦙ ⦙ •		seven
⦙ ⦙ ⦙ ⦙	8	ei ___ ght
⦙ ⦙ ⦙ ⦙	9	nine
⦙ ⦙ ⦙ ⦙ ⦙		ten

89

Summer
Math Game

The object of this math quessing game is to give each student a chance to figure out what number is taped to his or her back. Print numbers, up to 20, depending on student skill level, on a piece of paper—any size will do. Tape number to the back of a student, as shown. Have the student ask questions that can only be answered with a "yes" or "no" response, such as, "Is my number odd?" or "Is my number smaller than 7?" To add variety to the game, separate students in rows according to; even or odd, bigger than five, and less than five. Graph the results.

Summer Manipulatives
Plastic Spoon Garden

Decorate a flat block of earth-colored plastic foam with a craftstick or twig fence, as illustrated. Divide the "garden" into rows and label each row with "seed-packet" instructions on how many items to plant. Give students pots filled with spoon "flowers" and "vegetables" and plant in the garden, as directed. Use the garden again and again.

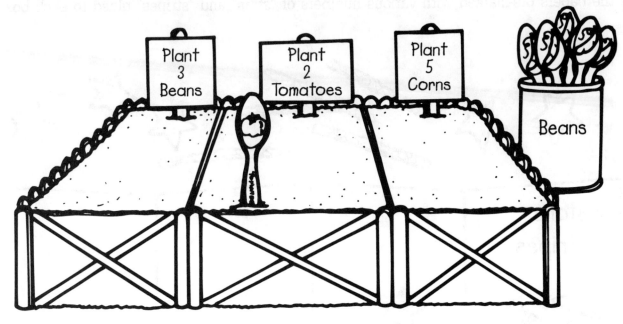

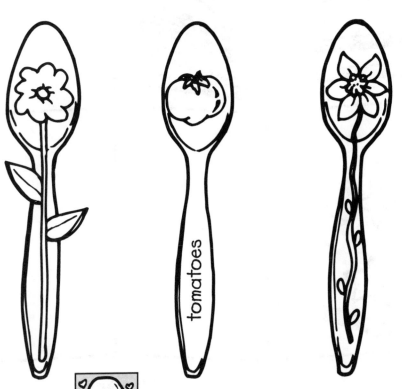

Create a "summer garden" full of fun objects to count. Decorate plastic spoons with permanent markers, stickers or cut paper, as illustrated. Store the decorated spoons in labeled containers or real flower pots. Place filled containers at each table to use with manipulative or graphing activities.

Reproducible

4th of July
Stars and Stripes Count

Use colorful pipe cleaners and foil or die cut stars to make patriotic manipulatives to practice counting and sorting skills. Cut red, white, and blue pipe cleaners into 1½" to 2" (3.9 cm to 5 cm) lengths. Place a box of stars and a box of "stripes" at each desk or station. Give each student a piece of paper either marked or folded into 8 boxes as illustrated. Offer instructions or have the papers pre-marked with various numbers of "stars" and "stripes" glued to each box.

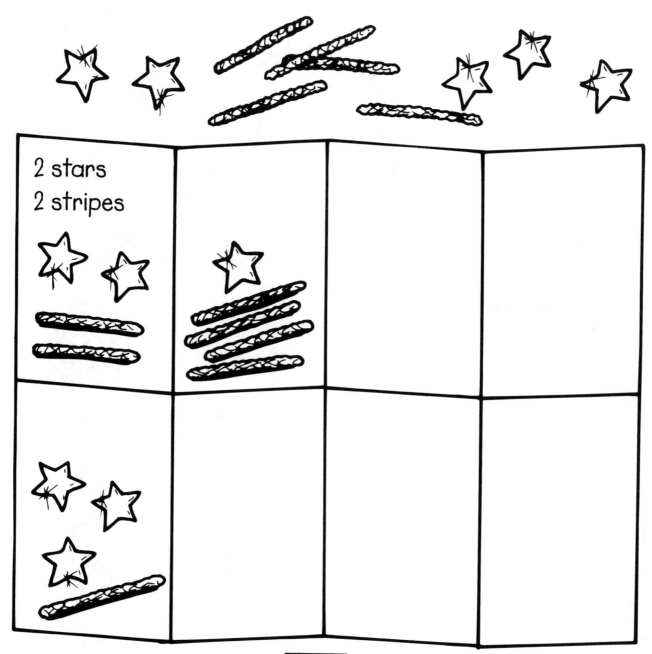

2 stars
2 stripes

Reproducible

4th of July
Bag of Stars

Use the star pattern below to create patriotic problems to sort and solve. Decorate a white or silver paper bag. Reproduce the star pattern, below and number each with a problem to be solved. Let the children solve the problems and sort star cards. Place all the "4" answers in the decorated bag, setting aside the other answers. This activity can be used with any other number or combination.

Is the answer 4?

Happy
4th
of July!

7 – 3

6 + 1

2 + 2

star pattern

Reproducible

Goldfish Cracker Estimate

Use snack time to practice estimating and counting skills. Place small bags of goldfish-shaped crackers* next to a small, blue paper plate lettered, as illustrated. Have each child write their estimates on a small piece of paper or napkin. Let children open their bags and count the "fish," writing the correct number of crackers on their plates—before sampling them. Answers and estimates may also be graphed.

* Activity can be adapted for older children by adding several different-shaped crackers to the bag.

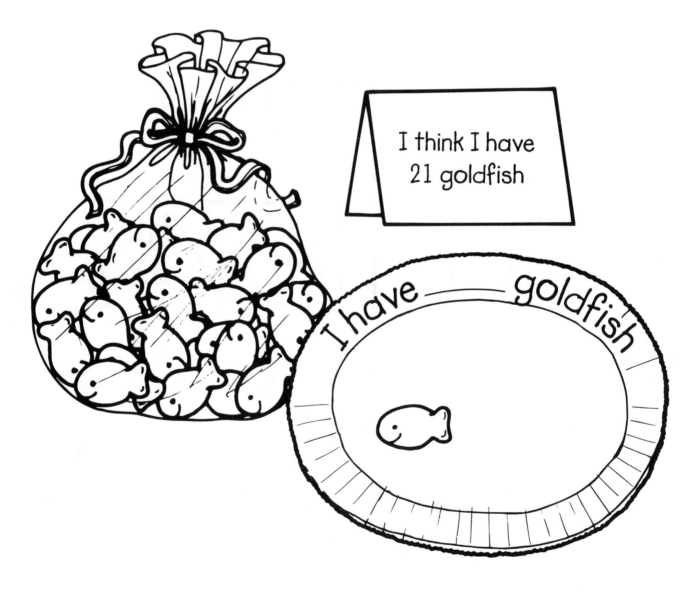

Summer
"Spot" the Dog

Can you draw the right number of spots on each dog?

6	 3 
8	 2 
4	 5 
1	 7 

Reproducible

Summer
Sea Shell Store

Set-up a "seashell" store to practice counting and using money. Reproduce the patterns below on heavy, colored paper. Laminate, if desired, and cut out. Label three boxes with assorted prices and put shells in each box, as shown. Give each student a "budget" or math problems to solve and "money" to buy the assorted shells. Use pretend coins and dollars.

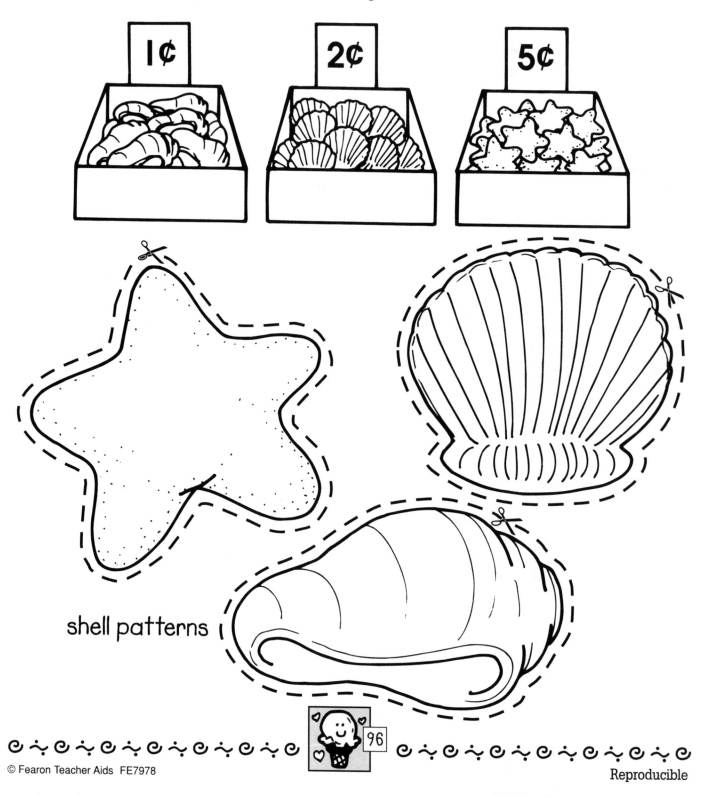

shell patterns

Summer

Picnic Summer Sets

Pack a summer picnic to practice counting and number sets. Decorate shoeboxes to look like picnic baskets, adding handles, "cloth" trim, as illustrated below. Number each box from 1 to 10, or as desired. Make "food" cards using stickers or illustrations from food ads or magazines. Vary the number of objects on each card. Place the completed cards and have the students sort the cards and put each in the basket that matches the number of items on the card.

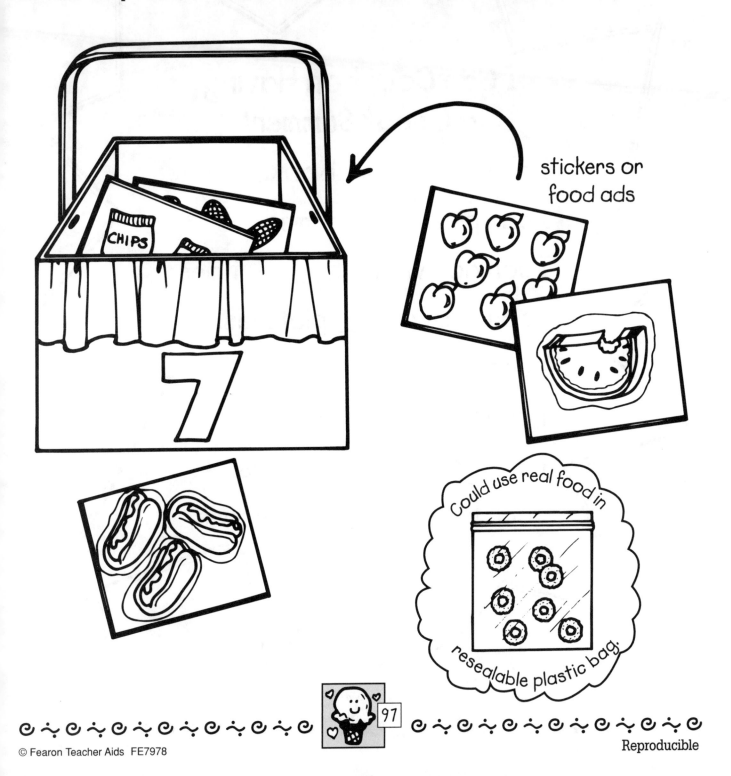

stickers or food ads

Could use real food in resealable plastic bag.

Reproducible

I Can Count on Having a Great Summer!

I can read _____ books.

I can play _____ games.

I can go swimming _____ times.

I can draw _____ pictures.

I can take _____ trips.

I can take _____ walks.

I can go on _____ picnics.

I can help with _____ chores.

98

End of Summer School
Pizza Party

Use an end-of-the-year pizza party to review several of the new math skills learned this past school year. Children will enjoy making their own custom minipizzas and eating them even more! (Peanut butter and jelly or cheese sandwiches could be used instead of pizza.) Be sure to have the children follow all hygiene and safety rules.

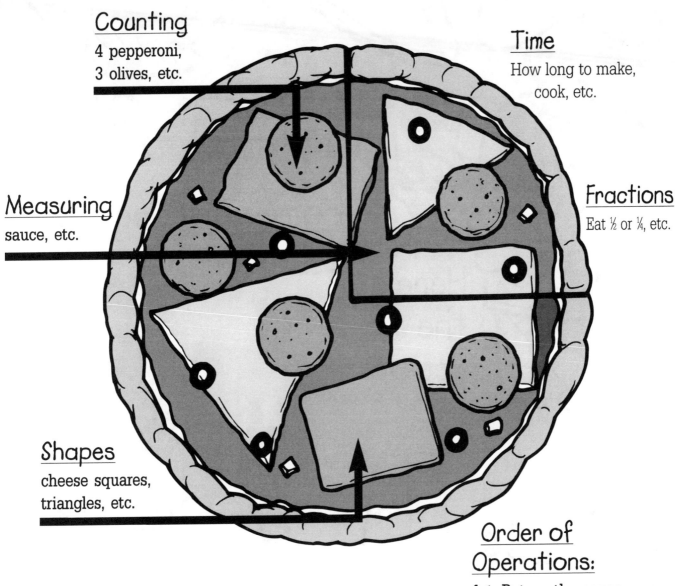

Counting
4 pepperoni,
3 olives, etc.

Time
How long to make,
cook, etc.

Measuring
sauce, etc.

Fractions
Eat ½ or ¼, etc.

Shapes
cheese squares,
triangles, etc.

Order of Operations:
1st: Put on the sauce.
2nd: Put on the cheese, etc.

99

Summer

Clip Art

+ − =

Here's the Scoop:

Math Homework Due:

Math is fun!

1 2 3
4 5 6
7 8 9
0 + −

100

Summer
Math Awards

Please review, sign, and return.
Thanks!

"Sea" what I can
do in Math!

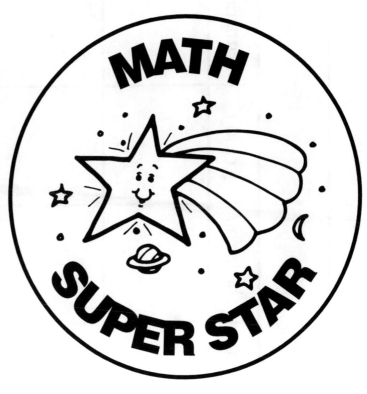

MATH
SUPER STAR

certificate

_____
name

is a "cool"
Math Student!

_____   _____
signed   date

101

Calendar Pattern

	Sunday	Monday	Tuesday	Wednesday	Thursday	Friday	Saturday

102

Clock Pattern

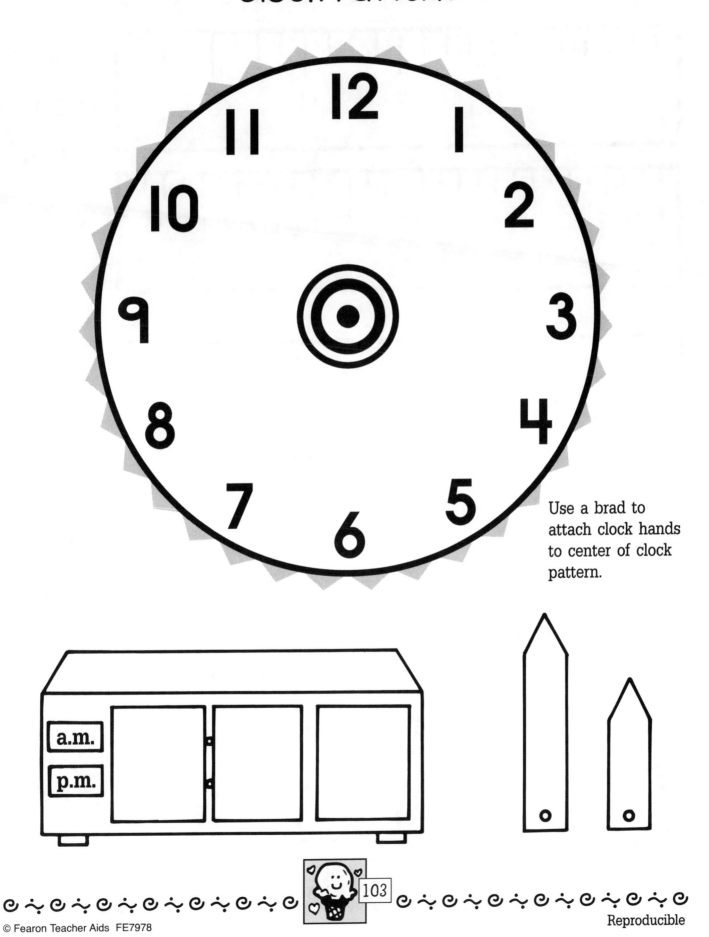

Use a brad to attach clock hands to center of clock pattern.

a.m.

p.m.

Reproducible

Measurement Patterns

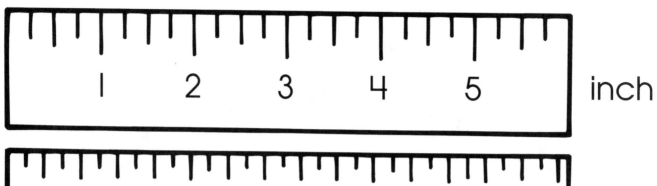

inch

cm

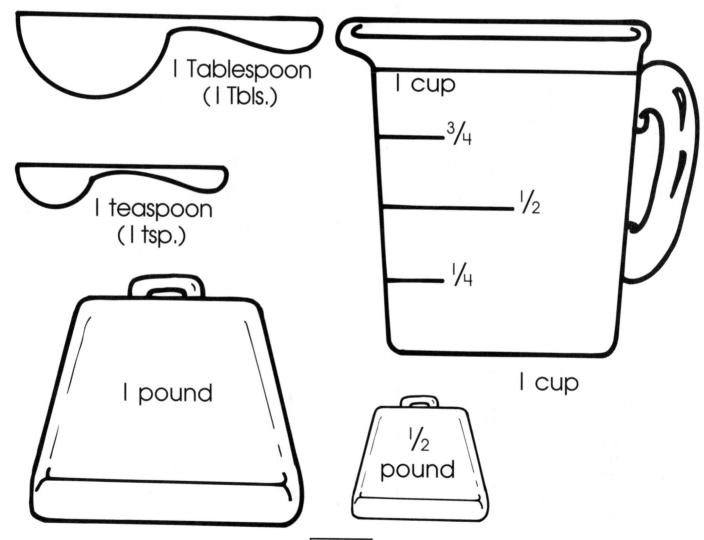

1 Tablespoon
(1 Tbls.)

1 teaspoon
(1 tsp.)

1 cup

¾

½

¼

1 cup

1 pound

½ pound

Measurement Patterns

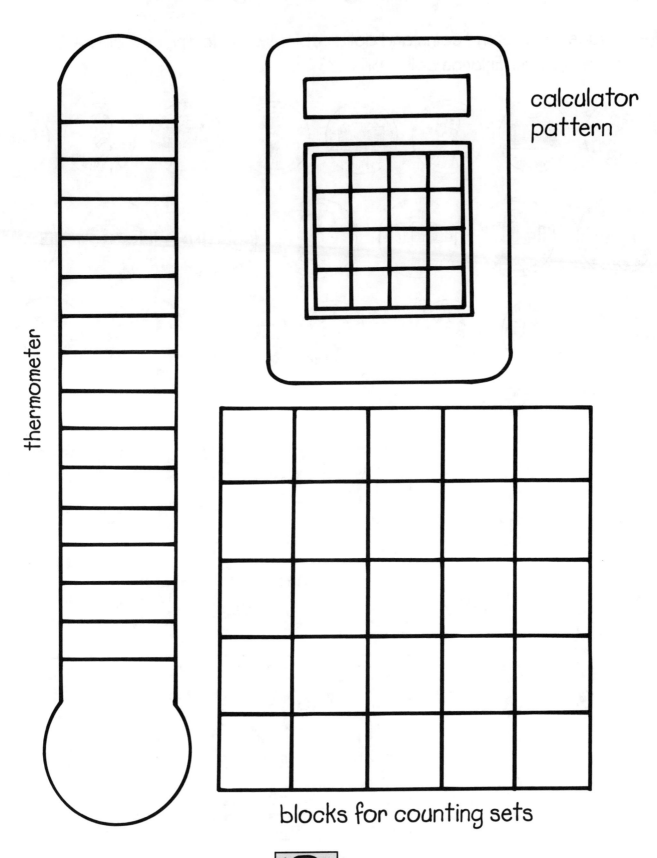

thermometer

calculator
pattern

blocks for counting sets

 105

Reproducible

Play Money

Reproduce the pretend coins and dollars, below, and laminate, if desired.
Coins are full size. Enlarge dollar bills 133%.

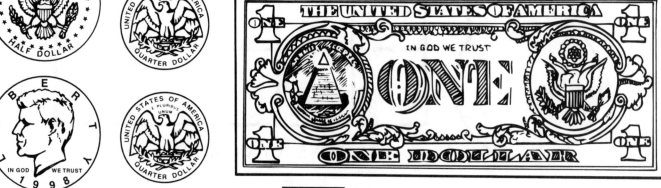

Reproducible